a year in the life of windsor and eton joanna jackson

a year in the life of windsor and eton joanna jackson

F

FRANCES LINCOLN LIMITED
PUBLISHERS

*To cousin Sue and all the rest
of my family – happy memories
of growing up in Windsor*

With thanks to Sue – thanks for help
with the State visits; the organisers of
the Royal Horse Show and the Royal
Tattoo; the helpful and charming
swan uppers; the staff at the swan
sanctuary; all at the Guards Polo
Club; the staff at the Royal Airforce
Memorial and The Carriage Driving
Association.

Frances Lincoln Ltd
4 Torriano Mews
Torriano Avenue
London NW5 2RZ
www.franceslincoln.com

A Year in the Life of Windsor and Eton
Copyright © Frances Lincoln Limited 2011
Text and photographs copyright ©
Joanna Jackson 2011
First Frances Lincoln edition 2011

British Library Cataloguing-in-Publication data
A catalogue record for this book is available from
the British Library.

ISBN: 978-0-7112-2936-5

Printed and bound in China

9 8 7 6 5 4 3 2 1

OPPOSITE: The Household Cavalry
on ceremonial duty.
PAGE1: The Round Tower at night.
PAGES 2–3: Windsor Castle.

contents

windsor and eton introduction

Royalty, railway and river are the important 3 'R's as far as the town of Windsor is concerned. Over the last thousand years or so they have moulded and shaped the town and will probably continue to do so for the next thousand.

There had been a royal presence in the area for many years before William the Conqueror arrived and built the castle that was to have such an impact on the town. The old Saxon kings had a settlement where Old Windsor now stands, drawn to the area by the good hunting to be found in nearby Windsor Forest.

The oldest known continuously inhabited part of the town is the area known as Clewer – Saxon for cliff dwellers. They presumably lived in the chalk cliff on which the castle now stands. The oldest building still standing in the town is the church of St. Andrew in Clewer whose walls and famous peapod font are of Saxon origin. Windsor's oldest byway is Peascod Street, named after Peas Croft, a medieval field, which was at the gateway to the river crossing which linked the forest and the castle. Peas were a local crop of great importance at the time.

After the castle was built, the area immediately around it grew in importance. There is a Fish Street and a Butcher's Row the names of which suggest that trading grew on the back of the population increase which occurred when the Royal Court came to town. The houses around the castle date back to the seventeenth century and this cobbled area has become a honey pot for the many tourists that swarm to the town. Of the many attractions, the leaning Market Cross House; Queen Charlotte Street (the shortest street in England at just 51 feet, 10 inches long); and a house in Church Street marketed as the home of Nell Gwynn, the most infamous mistress of the philandering King Charles II, are the highlights. The Guildhall built by Windsor resident Sir Christopher Wren stands proudly next to the parish church and provides the town with a registry office which marries the famous, infamous and not-so-famous. Elton John married David Furnish, and Prince Charles married Camilla there. Every day in the summer the band marches up the road accompanying the soldiers changing the guard. Locals know what time to avoid the centre of town! Although Windsor's numbers swell hugely in the summer there is a steady trickle of tourists all year round making it a busy, bustling place with great shopping as well as sightseeing.

Surprisingly horses are the other hugely influential factor in Windsor life. They feature in so many aspects of life in the town. The racing at Ascot and Windsor, Windsor Horse Show, the Royal Tattoo, the Household Cavalry, the polo

The Irish Guard.

and the carriage driving. It is helpful to like horses if you live in Windsor!

Across the river the delightful Eton village, dominated by historic Eton College, is full of quaint shops and cafés. Both Eton and Windsor are surrounded by wonderful countryside providing miles of walking for those not on horseback. The park is a vast space to enjoy with areas of wilderness and sympathetic cultivation of great beauty alike. You can walk along the Thames River path from Eton through fields to Dorney Lake (home of the rowing events in the 2012 Olympics) with its own wonderful arboretum. Windsor is a fantastic place whether you live there or just come to visit.

The chapel, Eton College.

winter

Windsor Castle from the Brocas.

early days

In the days of the Saxon kings, pre-1066 and all that, there was a manor house in Windlesora a few miles down river from where Old Windsor now resides. This manor house was located next to a forest that provided great hunting – the pursuit of kings.

The manor house was used regularly by Edward the Confessor and the name Windlesora means 'a riverbank with a windlass'. A windlass was a contraption that was used to haul cargo up from a river boat. Its presence in the name suggests that there was a trading station on the site.

Edward, as an old man, knowing he had no natural heirs seemed to delight in promising his crown to all and sundry. He had lived in Normandy for many years and knew 'William the Bastard' well. 'William the Bastard' was the illegitimate son of Robert I, Duke of Normandy. He is better known to us as 'William the Conqueror'. He claimed he had been promised the English crown by Edward in 1051. Harold, Earl of Wessex also claimed that Edward had promised him the English crown. These two claimants' rival armies met at the Battle of Hastings and William was the victor. He was crowned William I in Westminster Abbey on Christmas Day, 1066. This event had huge implications for England and of course Windsor.

When Edward died he had left the manor house and its surrounding forest to Westminster Abbey. William bought them back because "the place seemed suitable…a forest fit for the chase and diverse other things that are proper for kings".

Prior to 1066 England had been divided into different kingdoms. Now William controlled them all but it was hard work keeping all the rebellious subjects under control. All over the country little fortresses were built. Around London he built a circular series of fortresses about a day's march from each other with the Tower of London in the centre. About two miles from his manor house there was a chalk escarpment, a hill by a river was a very suitable place for one of his Norman motte and bailey style fortresses. This consisted of a round tower on a mound with fortified enclosures around it. The structures at this time would have been made of wood but were later updated into stone buildings. The Windsor Castle we know today was one of the ring of castles originally built by William, with the Tower of London the only other survivor.

Henry I, William's son, moved the court from the old Saxon manor to the new castle and the name followed. The Saxon village became Old Windsor and a new Windsor grew up below the castle.

William was also responsible for the Domesday Book an eleventh century version of a national census. It was an immense undertaking logging land, livestock and wealth owned by all his subjects. This knowledge was a tool to help him raise subsequent taxes. It was completed in 1087 and includes entries for Clewer, Dedworth, Windsor and Eton.

St. Andrews Church, Clewer. Thought to be Windsor's oldest building.

The Curfew Tower at Windsor Castle where historically, bodies of the executed were hung as a warning to others. For centuries it was known as Clewer Tower.

Runnymede in the snow.

eton

In 2010 David Cameron won a tightly fought General Election with a minority Conservative Party and after five days of behind doors negotiation became the nineteenth Old Etonian to become Prime Minister of Great Britain, forming a ground breaking coalition government with the Liberal Democrats. What is it about this school, which visually resembles a combination of Hogwarts and Gormanghast, and is about the size of an inner city comprehensive that makes it able to churn out British prime ministers and politicians with such regularity? Twelve of the Conservative politicians on Cameron's front bench are from Eton as is Boris Pffile Johnson, the Mayor of London, as well as five of the fresh faced newly elected MPs. It's not only politicians that have recently emerged from Eton and become movers and shakers. Contemporaries of David Cameron in the 1970s and 1980s included actors Damien

Lewis, and Dominic West, explorer Bear Grylls, Olympic rowers Matthew Pinsent and Ed Coode, three day eventer William Fox-Pitt and food writers and presenters Hugh Fearnley-Whittingstall and Tom Parker Bowles. It is famously a school of enormous privilege and wealth, but it goes far beyond that with the education which it offers.

Boys' names are put down at birth for the right to attend the school but these days an exam has to be passed at thirteen to cement a place on top of which a fee of around £30,000 a year is paid until the boys leave at the age of eighteen. It was not always thus. King Henry VI founded the school in 1440 as a place to educate poor but bright students in preparation for transferring to King's College, Cambridge, also founded by the King, to continue their education. It originally had seventy King's Scholars who were provided

The playing fields of Eton College where Wellington was claimed to have said the battle of Waterloo was really won.

for by the school which Henry endowed with a substantial income from the surrounding lands. It was not until later that they were joined by the Oppidans – the fee payers. Today the school is still divided into the Scholars and the Oppidans and their school uniform is still more or less the same. They wear tail coats and pin-striped trousers and look like ushers at a wedding. The top hats went out in the 1960s and fagging, the use of junior boys as servants to the seniors was abolished in the 1970s. Other peculiarities include the Wall Game – a game played only at Eton with rules so bizarre only players seem to understand them. Cricket is played by the 'drybobs' and rowing is for the 'wetbobs', terms are called 'halves' with three a year, the women who look after the boys are called 'dames', lessons are called 'schools', sixth formers are 'specialists' and prefects are members of 'Pop' and walk

round in a special uniform of colourful waistcoats and baggy trousers. Pop was originally a debating society, formed in 1811, that used to meet in Mrs Hatton's lollipop shop. Today about 1,300 boys attend the school.

Alan Clark the late diarist and rake, who also served as Defence Minister in Margaret Thatcher's government described Eton as "an early introduction to human cruelty, treachery and extreme physical hardship". Certainly there is much evidence of cruelty. Dr Keate, Headmaster from 1809–1834 had a reputation of being the greatest flogging headmaster. He took over at the end of the debauched Regency era when discipline was lax and behaviour was disorderly so maybe his floggings were justified. The flogging block over which boys were stretched and thrashed with a birch rod until they streamed with blood is to be seen in the school museum complete with the birch. Keate however had another side – he was a very good teacher and a fine orator and encouraged boys to deliver speeches with "clarity of voice". Two of his pupils went on to be prime ministers – Gladstone and Derby. Much emphasis has always been put on the importance of public speaking and debating which is almost certainly why so many Old Etonians end up acting, in the media or in politics.

The Classics, English Literature and Creative Writing are also massively encouraged with fruitful results. How many schools can boast a library with a section of first editions written by old boys? Percy Shelley, one of the major Romantic poets, engraved his initials on his desk when a pupil. Shortly after World War I Aldous Huxley, author of *Brave New World*, taught French to George Orwell, author of *1984* and *Animal Farm*. All three books are considered modern classics. David John Moore Cornwall alias John Le Carre was also a teacher at Eton going on to write numerous spy novels, as did Eton pupil Ian Fleming who created the James Bond books. Guy Burgess went one better and became a spy himself – for the wrong side!

Going around the school itself and coming across the war memorial it also becomes apparent how many famous and brave soldiers Eton has produced. Like many private schools Eton has a very active Cadet Corps where pupils join the army, navy or airforce and learn to march, shoot, fly and generally become disciplined members of a combat team. David Cameron interestingly opted to do community service instead. Many Old Etonians go on to join the armed forces. An astonishing thirty seven old boys have received the Victoria Cross, Britain's highest medal for valiantry. Eton's most famous soldier has to be the Duke of Wellington who led Britain to victory at the Battle of Waterloo and later became yet another British prime minister. He is famous for saying – although he almost certainly didn't say it – "Waterloo was fought and won on the playing fields of Eton".

Throughout its illustrious history Eton has managed to produce a disproportionate number of famous people – politicians, writers, soldiers, actors, sportsmen, explorers and academics. However, surprisingly few scientists have emerged from its ranks – perhaps the pupils are too busy reading and debating to do experiments!

To many people, Eton epitomises all that is wrong with today's society celebrating elitism and the upper classes. Certainly little Eton High Street is a strange, surreal place with gentlemen's outfitters selling shooting outfits and morning suits, there is even a branch of the exclusive Coutts Bank, how many village high streets have one of those? But look a bit deeper into the philosophy of the teaching at the school and what emerges is a centre of excellence that encourages discussion and free thinking backed up by amazing facilities. It is just a shame that this excellence is not freely available to all – think of the potential of the country if the whole population could have an Eton education.

Snow covered statues, boys on a break from 'schools' (lessons) and the chapel as seen from the Thames.

Windsor and Eton at night.
ABOVE RIGHT:
The eyepiece on the bridge looking down Eton High Street.
LEFT: The Guildhall, designed by Sir Christopher Wren.
OPPOSITE: The Theatre Royal.

railways and roads

Millions of years ago, during the ice age, the massive glaciers came within twenty miles of Windsor. During the big thaw, ice melt water flowed to the sea with rivers carving their way through the landscape. As the rivers meandered along, areas of shallower water created crossing points and habitations evolved at these hubs of activity. Windsor and Eton were two such adjacent areas.

In ancient times the river was an artery of communication for transport and the movement of goods. It was easiest and cheapest to use a barge to move large items around the country. The stones used to build the original Windsor Castle were brought downstream from Oxford and upstream from Caen in Normandy. The kings and queens would often travel from London by boat to Windsor.

The first bridge joining Windsor and Eton, made from five large oak trees sourced from Windsor Forest, was first mentioned in 1169. By 1277 it was deemed unsafe for laden carts to cross. It was reinforced and to pay for repairs a toll system was introduced. Barges passing under the bridge had to pay as did carts crossing over the bridge. The toll was in place until 1898 when, after a three year legal battle, the Lords of Justice proclaimed the bridge toll free. The present bridge was built in 1822 but in the 1970s the heavy road traffic between Windsor and Eton put an intolerable strain on the infrastructure. The Windsor by-pass was constructed and the bridge was pedestrianised.

Living next to a river brings its advantages but it also has a downside – flooding. There are constant records of major flooding throughout the nineteenth century particularly affecting the poor people who lived in the slums at the bottom of the town and those across the river at Eton.

In the Victorian era, Windsor was full of contradictions. The wealth of the Empire was reflected by the many grand state visits to the castle and the town was always decorated lavishly for those occasions with dignitaries such as Napoleon III and the Russian Tsars passing through. Behind the grandeur though was abject poverty. A particularly deprived area arose where prostitution, gambling and violence was common. The infamous Clewer Ditch, an open sewer, travelled through the town to the river. At times of flood the contents of the ditch spewed out onto the streets causing regular outbreaks of typhoid and cholera. Prince Albert, although tucked away in his ivory tower, was not immune and succumbed to a bout of typhoid and died prematurely aged 42 in 1861. Child mortality in the town at the time was almost 50%. In 1838 a health inspector's report recorded that Windsor was the most unsanitary town in the country. During the floods life carried on with punts being used to get around and chairs with planks on them providing makeshift walkways.

The railway came to the rescue of the filthy town. The tradesmen wanted this new form of transport because they foresaw the opportunities that it could bring. The Crown and Eton College however were not so keen. An almighty row brewed. The land over which the track would pass was mainly owned by the two rich establishments opposing its building. The Crown feared intrusion into its privacy and pollution. The College headmaster believed that the pupils would be lured by the vice in London and be led astray. Eventually the townspeople triumphed and the Great Western Railway, Paddington-Windsor line arrived in October 1849. The famous engineer Isambard Kingdom Brunel designed the wrought iron 'bow and string' bridge, which is now listed

The old Great Western Railway Station,
now a shopping mall.

The many swans of Windsor collect at a popular feeding spot with the bridge joining Windsor and Eton in the distance.

as an architecturally significant development, and the long viaduct. To build the station the notorious slums near the castle walls had to be demolished and the residents were re-located in much better, more sanitary accommodation. The clean-up of Windsor had begun. The Queen also took to the railway, taking her first trip a month after it opened. The Prince wasn't as keen as his wife and travelled by horse and carriage deciding that travelling at forty four miles per hour was far too fast.

Another station at the riverside was also built by the South Western Rail Company. The walls have the letters VR (Victoria Regina) and PA (Prince Albert) built into the brickwork and seven arches with large double doors were built so that the Household Cavalry could ride their horses directly onto a special train for transportation to London.

These two railways transformed Windsor from a grubby, slum ridden backwater to a suburban town of some charm which became the tourist attraction it remains today. From the mid 1800s to the early 1900s the population of the town almost doubled from 11,217 residents to 20,301. The age of the commuter had arrived.

The coming of the railways saw the decline of the use of the river for delivering goods and it was used less and

less. The arrival of the car finally finished it off as a viable trade route. The first car journey in England passed through Windsor when in 1895 the Honourable Evelyn Ellis, a resident of nearby Datchet, drove a car from Hampshire to Datchet via Windsor. The first traffic jam was also recorded in Windsor when Edward VII held a grand garden party in 1905 and all his rich friends drove their new cars to the event. A freak occurrence then, so commonplace today!

Today the Thames is a source of pleasure and leisure and the nearby Jubilee River is a manmade river stretching from Taplow to an area downstream of Windsor just above Datchet. It was opened in 2002 to prevent Windsor and Maidenhead flooding. It worked beautifully for Windsor but the residents of Datchet and Wraysbury weren't so happy when a couple of years later all the excess water from heavy rains arrived on their doorsteps instead! The Great Western Railway station, now a grade two listed building, was converted into an up-market shopping area which today attracts many shoppers. The line connecting Windsor to Waterloo remains and together with the M3 and M4 brings hoards of tourists daily to see the sights of this historic town.

An Eton boy escapes the inclement weather.
OPPOSITE: Queen Victoria, not amused by the snow!

The firs of Valley Gardens and
an ice-covered Wick Pond.

ABOVE: The main lake of Virginia Water on a beautiful winter's morning.
BELOW: The Thames at Runnymede.

Snow covered Runnymede.

the great park

The Great Park, as it is known locally, is one of the finest landscapes in Britain containing some of the oldest Oaks in the world. It dates back to the time of the Norman conquest when William I came to Windsor and chose the eroded chalk cliff on the north boundary of the park on which to build his fortress – the site of today's Windsor Castle. The park is divided into three distinct geological types. The top end is a 100 metre layer of London clay lying on top of a thick layer of chalk, the middle is loam and at the bottom end the chalk, clay and loam are covered with bagshot sand. The clay and loam provide a rich soil, perfect for farming and ancient trees. The acidic but well drained soil of the south however, provides a fantastic environment in which to plant all the exotics from the east, brought back by the Victorian plant hunters from their travels to places such as the Himalayas and Japan. Azaleas, rhododendrons and acers thrive here in the Valley Gardens, Saville Gardens and Virginia Water, today collectively known as the Royal Landscape.

The park was originally known as Windsor Forest and covered an area of land far greater than today's park. Then, a forest was not the wooded area we associate the word with today. In medieval times a forest was an area of heath, grassland and wetland with the occasional copse that supported deer and other game, was designated as such by the King and was subject to forest law. By the late twelfth century almost a third of southern England was classified as Royal Forest and was under forest law. Understandably this law was hugely unpopular as it prevented local people

Snow covered rhododendrons in Valley Gardens.
OPPOSITE: The Great Park.

from grazing their animals, collecting firewood or catching food for their own consumption unless special dispensation had been awarded. Dogs had to have their claws removed so that they could not hunt. Anyone caught breaking the law was liable to suffer extreme punishment such as blinding, castration or execution. It is from this era that the legend of Robin Hood grew, a common man stealing from the rich and giving to the poor and living in a forest. The uprising of the barons was partially brought about by the draconian Forest Law, and the Magna Carta, signed locally at Runnymeade, forced the King to relinquish some of his authority over the forest lands. Gradually the law became less important and remained dormant until the time of Charles I when, in need of money, he exercised some of his old rights. It was partly these actions that increased his unpopularity to the point of civil war, when he ultimately lost his head. So forest law has had a part in the downfall of two kings. There has never again been any serious attempts to resurrect forest law.

The Normans loved to hunt and introduced both fallow deer and rabbits into Britain to add to their hunting entertainment. Hunting was however, far more than just

a hobby. It was training in horsemanship for warfare and a pastime during which status and honour were established and where members of the court competed for proximity to the monarch. It was not without danger, with Richard the Conqueror losing two sons and a grandson in hunting accidents.

Deer have been a constant in the park except for a short period of time during and after World War II when they were removed to Balmoral in Scotland so that the park could be used for food production for the war effort. They returned in 1979 in an enclosed area at the suggestion of Prince Philip, the park ranger.

Today the Great Park is mainly used for recreational purposes and the public are free to wander over most of it. When driving to Windsor along the A308 the road crosses a part of The Long Walk with the castle at one end and the Copper Horse statue standing proudly on top of Snow Hill at the other. The Long Walk was originally commissioned by Charles II in 1680 and was designed more as a vista than for walking along. In the style of the French landscape gardener Le Notre who had designed large areas of Versailles, it

Virginia Water Cottage
and its boathouse.

epitomised a royal landscape of the time. It wasn't until 150 years later that the Copper Horse was added to the vista. Built by George IV, it is a statue depicting his father George III and carries a Latin inscription which translated reads 'Best of Fathers'. Ironically they had an appalling relationship! No one will ever know why he decided to honour his father in this way but it has left Windsor with a dramatic statue at the end of a very dramatic walk. The statue itself is not copper but bronze and it was delivered to its resting place in bits and assembled on site. Apparently sixteen of the men assembling it got inside the giant horse and had their lunch – presumably sheltered from the wind.

Another well known and frequently visited area of the park is Smith's Lawn. A lawn was originally a glade or pasture in a deer park not a beautiful grassy area that we think of today. This area was originally heath land covered with heather. During World War I it was used as a military camp, to begin with for soldiers about to go to war, and at the end of the war for the Canadian Forestry Corps who came over from Canada, specially requested for their tree felling skills. The

war effort desperately needed timber. Originally shipped from Canada the transportation ships became targets of u-boats and so the lumberjacks came to England instead and felled thousands of ancient trees, changing the landscape dramatically. After World War I the area was used as an airstrip and during World War II it was used by both the American and the Royal Air Forces. After World War II the area became the home of the Household Brigade Polo Club later renamed the Guards Polo Club. It remains the largest polo ground in Europe today.

The park is very large and there are many roads within it with a unique speed limit. It was suspected that when Britain decimalised their coinage that miles would give way to kilometers in the not too distant future. This however never happened so the speed limit in the park remains the unusual 38 mph in preparation for being 50 kph.

The park today is a beautiful space which to enjoy in such close proximity to the capital city, and helps make Windsor a very special place.

spring

The enormous ceremonial Royal Standard
flown on special occasions such as the
Queen's birthday on 21 April.

windsor horse show

In 1943 with the United Kingdom in the middle of the bloody World War II, a national campaign called 'Wings for Victory' was launched to raise funds for RAF aircraft. Count Robert Orssich and Geoffrey Cross decided to help this war effort by holding the first 'Windsor Horse and Dog Show' and with the glamour of royal patronage it proved to be a huge success with almost £400,000 being raised to help the cause. Due to its popularity the show has continued annually ever since. The 'dog show' part of the event however only lasted for one year due to a rather unfortunate event involving the poor Count, his lurcher dog and King George VI's chicken drumstick. The dog left the scene happy but subsequently dogs were banned from the show.

Over the years many members of the Royal Family have competed in various categories. In the inaugural 1943 show the young Princess Elizabeth won the single driving turnout class, she also competed with her sister Margaret the following year. Later her daughter Princess Anne would compete in the show jumping events and her husband Prince Philip in the carriage driving.

It is the largest horse show in the country lasting five days, and during that time more than 20 tonnes of manure is deposited and removed from the site! Originally held in the public Home Park it was moved in 2005 to the private area of the park because of regular problems with drainage with flooding during heavy rain leading to delays and cancellations over the years. The rugby players and cricketers who had their playing surfaces dug up by galloping horses were grateful of the move. The ground is now permanent and situated in the shadows of the castle, which is lit at night for the duration of the show. It is in a magnificent setting and the Queen has the luxury of just popping out of her house any time to see what is going on in her back garden! She visits informally most days with one of the Royal Family attending the Royal Tattoo in the evening in an official capacity.

The Windsor Royal Tattoo was started in 2008 to raise funds for the Royal British Legion, best known for their poppy campaign in November, who provide financial support for injured soldiers. It was the inspiration of Simon Brookes Ward the horse show organiser and an ex-serviceman himself. The show highlights the work of the soldiers of today in theatres of war such as Afghanistan but also has entertainment such as the musical ride of the Household Cavalry and the Massed Bands of the British Army. It is a grand spectacle which is enjoyed by many thousands of people.

LEFT: Horse boxes parked in Home Park.
RIGHT: Inspection time.
OPPOSITE: Show jumping in the main
arena with the castle as a backdrop.

The King's Troop of the Royal Horse Artillery
perform their musical drive at the
Windsor Royal Tattoo.

Beautiful blossom trees line both sides of King Edward VII
Avenue and Home Park.

The wonderful bluebell walk at Clevedon.

Bluebells in the Great Park.

the royal landscape valley garden

Sandwiched between Smith's Lawn to the north and Virginia Water Lake in the south, Valley Garden is an informally planted oasis of splendour where the imported trees and shrubs blend naturally into the undulating hills of the original landscape.

This area was originally such a jungle of uncontrolled vegetation that the men employed to transform it labelled it 'Upper Burma'. This work was started after the end of World War II and many of the men were recently de-mobbed from service in the Far East and were used to chopping their way through jungle. A large area of land was cleared but many of the ancient trees were retained so that continuity between the old and the new was retained. The work was overseen and inspired by Sir Eric Saville who did a marvelous job of filling the area with plants that he begged and borrowed from major collectors in the poverty stricken times following the war. Azaleas and rhododendrons thrive in the sandy, acid soil and one of the highlights of the year is the fantastic display, in May, of blowzy colour performed by the azaleas in an area known as the Punch Bowl. It is here that most of the 'Wilson fifty' Kurume azaleas can be found. Ernest Wilson was a British plant collector who at the turn of the twentieth century discovered these beautiful plants being cultivated on a small island in the south of Japan. He chose his fifty favourites out of the many hundreds available and returned with them to the UK. They are now known as the 'Wilson fifty'.

The year's flowering starts in January with the highly perfumed yellow flowers of the hamamelis, followed by the mahonias, camellias and magnolias. In the long sweeping valleys thousands of daffodils provide great swathes of yellow, dotted later with the bright blue of the English bluebell. In the summer the late flowering rhododendrons and hydrangeas provide the colour and on into the autumn when the richly coloured, over-the-top, acers stand out amongst the muted oranges of our native trees. In 1954, a heather and dwarf conifer garden was created within the Valley Garden and close by is the pinetum an expanse containing specimens of various conifers.

The Valley Garden is a wonderful space to wander in whether you are really 'into' plants and gardening or not. It is just a very special place thanks to Sir Eric Saville.

Magnolia in Valley Garden. OPPOSITE: The Devil's Punchbowl – Valley Garden.

Dramatic displays of daffodils
in Valley Garden.

Buttercups on the Brocas.

Abundant spring flowers on the towpath.

Hawthorn dangles over the river.
OPPOSITE: A lovely old fence on the
towpath opposite Windsor Racecourse.

Although part of the Royal Landscape that includes the Valley Garden and Virginia Water, Saville Garden is a distinct entity. Enclosed and with its own magnificent entrance, you have to pay for the pleasure of seeing the delights within its boundaries.

The garden was the creation of Sir Eric Saville who was appointed Deputy Surveyor of Windsor Great Park in 1931. Saville was inspired by his mother who herself was a keen landscape gardener. He went to Cambridge and shared lodgings with Owen Morshead who later became the Librarian at Windsor Castle. The two remained friends with Eric often visiting Owen at Windsor, a time which fostered Saville's intimate knowledge of the area. After serving in World War I he returned to work in the family firm – Savilles Estate Agents gaining experience in estate management. When he got the appointment in the park he was both surprised and delighted and set to work transforming a small area to the south east, originally called Bog Garden, into the splendid garden it is today.

The original garden was a fraction of the size of today's. The planting was very natural and always in groups of odd numbers so not to look too formal. Natural features such as streams and undulations were incorporated into the overall design. The garden grew and gardens began to appear in gardens so today you can wander through the Golden Jubilee Garden, the Rose Garden, the Dry Garden and the New Zealand Garden to name but a few.

To enter the garden you have to pass through the award winning Saville Building. This was opened in June 2006 and is a triumph of modern architecture both aesthetically and practically. Its gridshell construction was inspired by the strength and beauty of a seashell and uses the latest technology. The design resembles a leaf and the building is made from larch and oak sourced locally, mainly from the park itself.

The gardens were renamed The Saville Gardens in 1951 in honour of the man whose vision had been realised in the 1930s and whose garden has been enjoyed by generations of people ever since.

The award winning Saville Building.
OPPOSITE: The interior of the roof.

all the kings horses and all the kings men

For over a thousand years soldiers have been inextricably linked to the town of Windsor. For as long as Windsor has had its castle there has been a military presence. This has helped to shape and define the area, with the local people living with the knowledge that many of their town's residents perish in wars overseas leaving their families behind to mourn. Windsor residents are far more aware than most of the sacrifices made by the armed forces in battlefields all over the world.

In the tenth century William the Conqueror's French knights commandeered the land owned by the local Saxons. They built the original motte and bailey castle and then built a garrison to defend it. Soldiers have been a constant part of the town life ever since. Sometimes more welcome than others.

During the Civil War between Cromwell and King Charles I, Windsor became a headquarters for the Parliamentarians. The townspeople were sympathetic to the cause but billeting hundreds of soldiers put an intolerable strain on resources and relations. Householders were obliged to feed and house the soldiers putting huge demands on their limited means. By 1644 the deer in the Great Park were almost wiped out from hunting to feed the swollen numbers living in the town. After the Civil War soldiers returned to Windsor for work and payment. The money ran out and the men went hungry and for a time Windsor became a lawless and dangerous place. King Charles I was beheaded in London but his body and his head were returned to Windsor where they were re-united with each other, being sewn together on a kitchen table before the whole body was buried in St. George's Chapel. After ten years of the republic the monarchy was restored and Windsor Castle became a Royal residence again. However 300 soldiers remained billeted at local inns and houses.

It was about this time that the mounting of the guard started and it continues to this day. Daily in the summer and on alternate days in the winter, at eleven o'clock in the morning, infantry soldiers march from their barracks through the town to change the guard at the castle. They are normally accompanied by a band of pipes and drums but when the Queen is in residence it is a full band. The streets are shut to traffic and the tourists and locals alike watch the procession before carrying on with their days. It is one of the highlights of a visit to Windsor. It is possible to tell whether the Queen is in residence by glancing up at the flag flying on the flagpole in the round tower. Most of the time the Union Jack is to be seen but when the Queen is in residence the Royal Standard is the flag of choice. On special occasions, such as the Queen's birthday a huge Royal Standard 38 feet by 19 feet is hoisted by two men and flutters majestically in the wind above the town.

There are two barracks in Windsor the Combermere Barracks where the Cavalry regiments are quartered and the Victoria Barracks where the infantry regiments are housed with the latter dating back to 1798. There are five infantry regiments that rotate duties in Windsor. They are the Grenadier, Coldstream, Scots, Irish and Welsh Guards. Their outward appearance is very similar – red tunics, dark blue trousers and bearskins but there are subtle differences that give away which regiment they belong to. The Grenadier Guards have a white plume on the left side of their bearskins and the buttons on their tunics are arranged singularly. The Coldstream Guards have a red plume on the right side of their bearskins and the buttons appear in pairs. The Scots Guards have no plume and buttons in groups of three. The Irish Guards have a blue plume on the right and buttons grouped in fours and lastly the Welsh Guards have a green and white plume on the left with buttons grouped in fives.

Their bearskins weigh nearly a kilogram, are around 50 centimetres tall and are made from the fur of Canadian brown bears which is later dyed black. They are not to be confused with busbies (smaller hats worn by the King's Troop, Royal Horse Artillery). The infantry have worn them on ceremonial occasions since 1815. They were introduced as part of the uniform in memory of the victory over the French at the Battle of Waterloo. They are hot and heavy and must be very uncomfortable on a hot summer's day!

The Household Cavalry is made up of the Life Guards who wear scarlet tunics and brass helmets with long white plumes, the Blues and Royals who wear navy tunics and brass helmets with long scarlet plumes and the Royal Dragoon Guards. The Household Cavalry have a very important role to play on the days when state visits happen. These are grand affairs usually occurring in March or April when the Queen entertains foreign dignitaries. There is a procession through the town usually from the station, up the hill through the town entering the castle via the Long Walk. The spectacular royal carriages carry the Queen and her guests with bands playing and the Household Cavalry in full ceremonial dress providing the escort. These events draw great crowds and are very impressive to watch and be part of.

The soldiers that perform all these ceremonial duties are however, first and foremost fighting men regularly engaged in war zones around the world. All the regiments have recently been in Afghanistan and Iraq. It must be quite a change to go from one day being dressed in a fancy eighteenth uniform guarding a castle to being in fatigues fighting the Taliban.

The drum horse of the Household Cavalry.

Firing a salute at the Royal Tattoo.

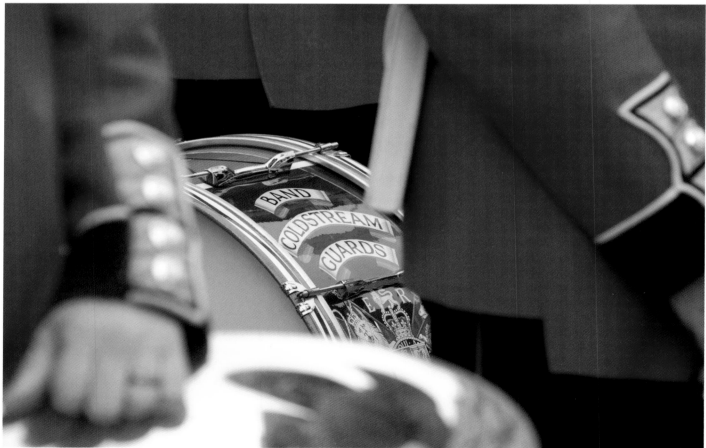

Soldiers from the Coldstream
and Irish Guards' bands.

Looking across the Thames towards
Windsor Racecourse.

The landing stage at Windsor Racecourse where punters disembarque for an evening of races at a summer meet.

summer

dorney rowing lake

For hundreds of years Eton boys have rowed on the River Thames next to the College. In the nineteenth century rowing, cricket and bathing were the summer sports with the latter being performed in the nude. To be eligible to row, a boy had to pass a swimming test, still a pre-requisite today.

'Swing, swing together,
With your backs between your knees'

The words above describe rowing and are taken from the famous 'Eton Boating Song' written by William Johnson Cory, a master at the school, for the 4 June celebrations of 1863. At that time Edmund Warre was also a master at the school going on to become headmaster between 1884 and 1905. Warre was an Old Etonian himself who had rowed at school and gone on to Balliol College, Oxford where he had continued his glittering record as an excellent oarsman. It was during his time teaching at Eton that he coached the boys and raised the profile of the rowing. Ever since then Eton has produced outstanding rowers. Sir Matthew Pinsent, Ed Coode and Andrew Lindsay are all Old Etonians and gold medallists at recent Olympic Games.

Annually, on the Wednesday closest to 4 June, Eton boys dressed in nineteenth century uniforms and row up the Thames in antique rowing boats to celebrate the birthday of King George III. The King was a patron and particular friend of the school and would visit regularly when in Windsor. The boys wear hats festooned in spring flowers and as they pass the school they stand up one by one in their precariously wobbly boats and when all upright, take off their hats in unison and

wave the flowers into the flowing water whilst saluting their Queen, country and school. This takes much skill and it is not unheard of for the whole boatful to end up in the water. At the following parent and student picnic everyone tucks into Eton Mess the delicious dessert made from meringue, strawberries and cream and created at Eton in the 1930s.

In the 1960s some of Eton's rowing teachers felt that it would be safer for the pupils to row on a still water rowing course away from the increasing river traffic. Much planning went into the development of Dorney Rowing Lake over the ensuing years and in 2006 a magnificent facility was officially opened. Its original purpose to provide a rowing lake for the school has been far exceeded and in 2012 it is to be the site of the rowing and kayaking events at the London Olympics.

However, the area is far more than a rowing lake. Every care has been taken to retain the natural beauty of the area with a nature conservation zone that includes wading pools

Armillary sphere and stone circle at Dorney Lake surrounded by oxbow daisies.

Wild flowers flourish on the banks of the Jubilee River.

swan upping

Once a year for the last 800 years Swan Uppers have been marking young cygnets on the Thames. The first written records of the event date back to 1186. Back in the tweflth century, young swans were considered a delicacy and were eaten at banquets and feasts. All swans were owned by the monarch who then gave loyal subjects the right to own some, with each family having their own mark. Every year the swans were rounded up and the young marked in the same way as their parents. Gradually, as the domestication of chickens, ducks and geese increased, the need for swan meat diminished. Today, apart from the crown, only three bodies have maintained their rights to own swans, they are the Ilchester family which owns the swannery at Abbotsbury in Dorset and two London livery companies, the Vintners and the Dyers who have been swan upping since being granted ownership rights in the fifteenth century. Historically, the Dyers would put one nick on their birds' beaks and the Vintners two, today they ring the birds. All unmarked birds belong to the crown.

During the third week in July, six skiffs, two from the crown and two each from the Dyers and Vintners, set out on the 79 mile journey up the river from Sunbury to Abingdon. When a new brood is spotted the uppers call out "all up" and the boats converge on and surround the family. The birds are captured and taken ashore where they are checked over, weighed and marked. The party is led by the Queen's swan marker who establishes the ownership, the swan markers of the respective companies being responsible for marking their birds.

Today the birds are not used for the table and swan upping is more an exercise in conservation. Many swans are still injured by fishing tackle although numbers have recovered since the 1980s when poisonous lead weights were banned, or the birds were used as shooting practice by youths with air guns. The local swan sanctuary is a charity in Eton and is full of injured birds, being rehabilitated for release back into the river. They work together with the Queen's swan marker to keep the swans on the Thames fit and healthy and the local children and fishing groups educated. When the Henley Regatta is on, the swans from that stretch of the river are caught and 'stored' at the sanctuary and returned home after the racing is over.

As the swan uppers pass Windsor Castle on their trip up-river, they stand to attention, and with oars raised salute "Her Majesty the Queen, Seigneur of the Swans".

The swan uppers row downstream in search of young unmarked cygnets.
BOTTOM LEFT: The Queen's swan marker, David Barber.

BELOW RIGHT: Swans recuperating at the swan sanctuary.
OPPOSITE: All the swan uppers in Boveney Lock.

Queen Anne's Ride.

The Castle as viewed through the mill stone on Queen Anne's Ride.

The boys of Eton College celebrate
George III's birthday.

horse racing

Horses were first domesticated in 4,500 BC. Since man started to ride he has raced. Both chariot and mounted horse racing were events in the ancient Greek Olympics by 638 BC. The sport became a public obsession in the Roman Empire and there is evidence that the Romans held races at Wetherby near York around 208 AD. During the age of chivalry, heavily armoured knights went off to fight the crusades. The knights' horses were heavy and slow, strong enough to carry the enormous weight of the armour. Abroad however, they came up against the agile Islamic fighters on quick, mobile Arab horses. The knights brought these horses back to Britain and began breeding a new, more athletic type of horse. The first recorded race meeting of these horses took place at Smithfield, London in 1174, during a horse fair.

Henry VIII was the first king to have a stud farm and he imported horses from Spain, France and north Africa. His descendants carried on this interest in developing the horse and continued to breed at the stud. James I built a palace at Newmarket and set up a racecourse nearby and today Newmarket is considered the home of British racing. Oliver Cromwell banned horse racing but with the re-introduction of the monarchy came the re-introduction of racing. Charles II is credited as being the 'father of the English turf'.

Originally races were over a four or five mile course. During meetings, other gambling events, such as cock-fighting, often took place. The crowds frequently became unruly, and to focus the public's attention back on the horse racing, the races were made shorter and more frequent. The Jockey Club was formed at Newmarket in 1750 to oversee and control English horse racing. A Jockey Club accountant, James Weatherby, was allocated the task of tracing the pedigree and compiling a family history of all the horses in England. Astonishingly, all Thoroughbreds alive today originate from three stud stallions. Byerley Turk (around 1680-1696), Darley Arabian (around 1700–1733) and Godolphin Arabian (1724–1753) are collectively known as the 'foundation sires'. Even more astonishing is that 80% of today's Thoroughbreds

come from Darley Arabian's great-grandson Eclipse who was born the year of the eclipse in 1764. He won eighteen races and because he was so good, other owners were so reluctant to race against him that eight of his races were declared walkovers! On his death he was dissected by vets desperate to find the secret of his success. They found a huge heart, powerful lungs and strong back legs!

There are two race courses in Windsor – Royal Ascot and Royal Windsor. Racing has been going on near Windsor for centuries with records of Charles II attending meetings on Datchet Mead but it was Queen Anne, the last of the Stuarts, who was responsible for the founding of the famous course at Ascot in 1711. Whilst out riding near the Great Park she came across heathland at East Cote that was perfect for 'horses to gallop at full stretch'. The first race meeting was held there on Saturday 11 August, 1711. The first four day meeting took place in 1768. This became a five day event in 2002 to celebrate Queen Elizabeth II's golden jubilee. The most popular day is known as Ladies' Day, where hats compete with horses for attention.

Royal Windsor racecourse held its first meeting in 1866. In 1926 Winston Churchill attempted to impose a betting levy. This was hugely unpopular and bookmakers at Windsor refused to accept bets causing the tax to be withdrawn. Later, in 1949, Churchill's horse Colonist II went on to win the 'Limetree Stakes' to rapturous applause. People quickly forgive and forget. The course is a figure of eight, one of only two such courses in the country. Meetings are held throughout the summer with the evening meets particularly popular with punters arriving by boat, the course being situated in glorious surroundings by the Thames.

The royal racing colours are a purple body with gold braid, scarlet sleeves and black velvet cap with gold fringe. These colours can be seen worn by jockeys racing on royal horses on both these courses throughout the season. Racing was originally a royal sport and it remains to this day a sport of kings (and queens).

Royal Ascot celebrates Ladies' Day known for its extravagant hats.
BELOW: The Queen accompanied by Prince Philip and Prince Andrew and other race goers on their way to Royal Ascot.

The Statue of Prince Christian Victor, Queen Victoria's grandson.

A statue of Prince Albert
on Smith's Lawn.

The cobbled streets near the castle are a magnet for tourists.

The tourist train.

The most crooked house
on the shortest street.

polo

Imagine yourself hurtling along at thirty miles an hour sitting precariously on top of half a ton of galloping muscle with an upturned walking stick in one hand, trying to hit a billiard ball through some goal posts. The date would have been 1869 and you would have been trying to play the new game of 'hockey on horseback' better known to us as polo. Cavalry officers tried out this new game at their barracks at Aldershot having read about it in *The Field* magazine – 'the game of kings, and the king of games' had arrived in England.

Rewind 4,000 years to when the tribes of central Asia domesticated wild horses. They migrated to Persia and mastered the art of warfare on horseback. At that time, often with teams of more than a hundred, a rudimentary game was played with sticks and a dead animal with the horsemen honing their riding skills for war. The first references to the game of polo are from Persian literature and date back to 600 BC, making it probably the oldest team game in the world. The cavalries of the Persian Empire conquered land from Constantinople in the west to as far east as Japan including China, India and Tibet (the word polo in fact is a derivation of the Tibetan word *pulu* meaning ball) and with them they took polo.

Although the game died out in China and Japan, the Indians continued to play the game in many provinces. During the British occupation of India, Joseph Sherer, a subaltern in the Indian Army witnessed the game being played in Manipur. Sherer and some fellow devotees went on to set up the Calcutta Polo Club which today holds the title of 'the oldest polo club in existence'. He wrote about it in *The Field* and it was this article that prompted the officer in the 10th Hussars at Aldershot to have a go. Within a short time it was part of British cavalry officers' training. It was however all rather chaotic, so in 1874 the Hurlingham Club established a set of rules. The British, like the Persians before them then took polo all around their empire.

James Gordon-Bennett, publisher and playboy, introduced polo to the USA in 1876. Over the next fifty years it flourished with in excess of 30,000 people attending international matches on Long Island. From 1900 to 1936 it was an Olympic sport. British cattlemen introduced the game to Argentina, which is now considered a mecca for polo aficionados.

Smith's Lawn in Windsor Great Park is the home of the Guards Polo Club formed in 1955 with the Duke of Edinburgh as its president. Matches are played there from April to September with the hugely popular Hurlingham Polo Association's International Day in July attracting over 20,000 visitors. Many famous people turn up for this event and attendance has become a must in high society's diary. Prince Charles was a regular polo player when younger, and his two sons William and Harry have carried on the family tradition. So it remains 'a game of kings, a king of games' even after 2,500 years.

Polo on Smith's Lawn. Cartier Day is a big social event with Argentina playing England.

Views of the river from
The Eye.

A view of the Thames Valley
at dusk.

Feeding the swans at sunset.

ABOVE: Dorney Court.
BELOW: Clevedon House.

ABOVE: Coldstream Guards prepare to change the guard.
BELOW: Irish Guards on horseback.
OPPOSITE: A Scots Guard with his ceremonial sword.

autumn

Autumn colours in the Valley Gardens.

air force memorial

War has always proved an enormous catalyst to the development of technology. Such was the case with the 'heavier-than-air' plane in World War I. The Wright brothers' inaugural flight in Kitty Hawk, North Carolina was in December 1903. Over the next few years gentle progress was made in the efficiency of aircraft but they remained flimsy machines made from wood and canvas that were notoriously unreliable and dangerous to fly. Up until 1914 there had not much enthusiasm from the British to invest in plane technology. Other European countries had been investing far more time and money into the machines. The Germans had developed an airship in the form of the Zeppelin and the Italians had been the first to use planes for military purposes in the Italian-Turkish war of 1911–12.

The start of World War I proved a turning point for the plane. The cavalry were rendered totally ineffective with the advent of trench warfare, and reconnaissance flights detailing the whereabouts of enemy troops and artillery positions became invaluable to the armies on the ground. To begin with, the idea of the plane as an offensive weapon was laughed at but something had to be done to stop the reconnaissance planes sending vital information back to their troops on the ground. The Frenchman Roland Garros attached a machine gun to the front of the plane in 1914 and in 1915 the Germans went one better by attaching a synchronised machine gun to their planes. The first offensive planes were used to shoot down reconnaissance planes but it wasn't long before the pilots were engaging in one on one dog fights. The German nicknamed the 'Red Baron' was probably the most famous fighter pilot of the time.

Although Britain had joined the race to develop an effective plane relatively late in the day, once all the country's great minds were engaged in the project, the country quickly caught up and ended the war with the best and most efficient air force in the world. The Royal Air Force was created on the 1 April 1918 just over six months before the end of World War I. Up until then the army had had its own air force, the Royal Flying Corps, and the navy its own, the Royal Naval Air Service. The bombing of London by Zeppelins in daytime raids in 1916 and the inadequate response of both these air divisions had focussed the minds of politicians who realised more resources and co-ordination must go into flying services. Eventually the two flying corps amalgamated into a new and separate service, the RAF.

By the time World War II started all three services were of equal importance with the RAF playing a vital role in the defence of Britain, especially during the heroic Battle of Britain. In total the war would cost the lives of 116,000 men and women of the air forces of the Commonwealth. Many of those were lost without trace and their graves are unknown. The memorial at Runnymeade commemorates those lost in operations from bases in the UK and north and western Europe. Their number totals more than 20,000 and their names are poignantly engraved on the walls of the memorial. The memorial is sited in a fantastic location at the top of Cooper's Hill in Runnymeade with panoramic views over the Thames Valley.

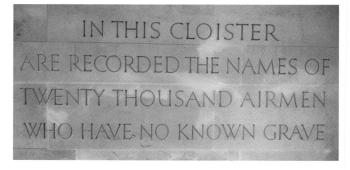

Details from the memorial.
OPPOSITE: The Royal Airforce Memorial, Runnymede.

Sunset over
Virginia Water.

The pinetum and high flyers
hill in Valley Gardens.

A view to Virginia Water from
the Plunket Pavillion.

Peter Townsend, a divorced older man who the church and the public considered unsuitable. By 2005 however, public opinion had changed enough to permit the divorced Prince of Wales, the future King Charles II, to marry the divorced Camilla Parker-Bowles. Three of the four children of the present queen are now divorced. How times change.

Edward VIII became the second king in the Windsor dynasty in 1936 on the death of his father, George V. He only reigned for 325 days and was never crowned, one of the shortest reigning monarchs in England's history. His father apparently once said that "after I am dead the boy will ruin himself within a year" how prophetic this proved to be.

He was a vain, rather immature man (he ignored royal protocol by having his profile on new minted coins facing left like his father. Normally the profile was alternated from left to right from one regent to the next but Edward thought his left side was more flattering than the right). At the time of his accession he was a single man with a reputation as a womaniser, preferring to have older, already married women as his mistresses. Then he met Mrs Simpson and everything changed. It was said of him that whilst "his predecessors were content with the prospect of a suitable mistress, he wanted an unsuitable wife". Up until this point in his life he had been unconventional and quite anti-establishment. Suddenly however, he met a woman he wanted to marry. In the eyes of the British people, he couldn't have chosen a more inappropriate woman if he had tried. Not only was she divorced (twice!) she was a commoner and even worse, a brash American! When he told Baldwin, the Prime Minister, of his intentions, he was given three choices – give her up, marry her and cause a constitutional crisis or abdicate – he chose the third option. A new dukedom was created for him – he became the Duke of Windsor.

The new Duke of Windsor moved to France, married Simpson and caused further scandal by visiting Hitler. It was suggested he had fascist German leanings although this was never proven. He only returned to England a couple of times in the 1960s. He died in 1972 and is buried at Frogmore; the Duchess is buried next to him.

Nearly twenty years later history nearly repeated itself with Princess Margaret, the Queen's sister when she expressed a wish to marry a divorced man, Group Captain Peter Townsend. The outcome however was different. When the love affair became common knowledge it was made clear to the Princess that if she married her lover she would have to renounce her royal rights, income and leave the country for at least five years. Unlike her uncle though she chose to toe the party line and issued a statement saying "I would like it to be known that I have decided not to marry Group Captain Peter Townsend. Mindful of the Church's teaching that Christian marriage is indissoluble, and conscious of my duty to the Commonwealth, I have resolved to put these considerations before any others".

During the abdication crisis public opinion was definitely not in favour of the marriage, however, the potential marriage between Princess Margaret and Peter Townsend split public opinion. Divorce was becoming much more common in society in general and therefore much more tolerated. When Charles and Diana divorced in 1996 it was not as shocking. What was shocking though was the public airing of their differences and affairs with both parties giving television interviews in which they divulged many intimate details of their private lives. Diana was such a popular personality that Charles could not compete. When she died tragically in a car crash in Paris in 1997 the House of Windsor hit its lowest point in public opinion.

More controversy followed. Charles' long term mistress Camilla Parker-Bowles was gradually introduced to royal duties after Charles' divorce. By this time the opinion of both the public and the Church had shifted to a point where civil marriage was seen as an acceptable solution. Initially Camilla was hugely unpopular but gradually, due to her dignified behaviour, the British public has warmed to her.

The family seems to have a new asset in Prince William who is apparently charming, and like his mother at ease with the public. Despite changing times the House of Windsor looks set to flourish and continue adapting and evolving as society demands.

The Jubilee Statue of Queen Elizabeth II at the end of Queen Anne's Ride.

The carriage driving championships held in the Great Park with the castle and the Copper Horse as a backdrop.

magna carta

On 10 June 1215, on the muddy banks of the River Thames at Runnymeade, King John signed and sealed a document that would become one of the most important documents in the history of England. It gave the power of taxation to Parliament (then, the Great Council), the Church was given freedom from royal interference, all weights and measures were made uniform throughout the kingdom, and most importantly every citizen was given the right to due legal process which led to trial by jury.

Why did a king give away so much of his power? King John was not an enlightened king who thought the document progressive and democratic and good for the kingdom, he only signed it because he was forced to by his powerful barons. He had no intention of ever fulfilling its obligations and was probably plotting to renege on the deal as he signed it. As fate would have it though he died very shortly after he put his seal to it, contracting dysentery following an orgy of gluttony.

Remember back to the tales of Robin Hood when Richard the Lionheart was away fighting crusades leaving his evil brother John, Sheriff of Nottingham, running the country. Although Robin Hood was a fictional character the other two were definitely real. Richard the Lionheart was a flamboyant character who got away with subjecting his people to exorbitant taxes because of his gallant persona. When he died his brother John became king. He kept up the high taxation but lacked Richard's charisma.

During his reign of sixteen years he managed to alienate nearly everyone. He fell out with the Pope over who should be Archbishop of Canterbury, and was subsequently excommunicated. He invaded France but failed to conquer the lands he was after. He quarreled with his Barons over his methods of ruling the country and most importantly the taxes he levied were extortionate.

The barons took up arms against him and captured London in May 1215 and in June the same year, dressed in full armour they descended on King John at Windsor Castle. He agreed to a meeting at Runnymeade. Runnymeade had, in Anglo-Saxon times, been a regular site for the country's leaders to congregate for discussion. *Runny* was the Anglo-Saxon word for meeting place and *meade* for meadow. Daily, the barons would come from Staines and the King from Windsor until they had thrashed out the wording of 'the great Charter' or 'Magna Carta'.

King John went back on his word almost immediately which led to the Barons War. The barons wanted to put the French Prince Louis on the throne but before this could happen John died so they abandoned Prince Louis in favour of the nine year old son of King John who was crowned Henry III. He ruled for fifty six years and during that time the Magna Carta was refined and retained and became the document on which English law was based and the source of important legal concepts found in the American Constitution and Bill of Rights.

So King John's over indulgence saved England from a French King, a bloody civil war and gave us the principles of no taxation without representation and the right to a fair trial under the law. His greed did us all a favour!

At the bottom of Cooper's Hill on land owned by the National Trust stands a monument to the signing of the Magna Carta. It takes the form of a classical temple and contains a pillar of English granite on which is written 'To commemorate Magna Carta, symbol of Freedom under Law'. It was built by the American Bar Association with money donated by 9,000 American lawyers. The unveiling ceremony in 1957 was attended by American and English lawyers alike.

The memorial of the signing of the Magna Carta at Runnymede.

virginia water

There was always a stream running through the area now known as Virginia Water but it wasn't until the Duke of Cumberland became the park ranger and decided to alter the landscape that the stream became a lake. The Duke was the favourite son of George II and a soldier of some note. Famous for orchestrating the massacre of Scottish forces at the battle of Culloden he was nicknamed 'Butcher Cumberland'. After his military career ended he went to live in Cumberland Lodge in the Great Park.

Landscape gardening at the time was undergoing a transition from favouring the controlled and formal garden, to the natural garden, embellished by numerous follies. Cumberland's brother and father had already transformed their estates in Richmond and Kew, which would later combine to become Kew Gardens, and he followed suit in Windsor beginning the transformation of this part of the park.

In the mid 1800s he had the river dammed and created the largest manmade lake of its time. Cumberland died a relatively young man at the age of forty four after years of over indulgence. A large obelisk was erected by his father in his memory and stands just outside the Saville Gardens. The inscription on the memorial with the word 'Culloden' in it was later altered by Queen Victoria omitting the mention of the infamous battle of which she was supposedly ashamed.

A few years after his death a massive summer storm caused the dam at the end of the lake to be breached and the subsequent flood water took the lives of several locals. George III took it upon himself to rebuild the lake and several promenades so it was and still is possible to stroll all around the beautiful area. There remain in the far right hand corner of the lake two of the original follies – The Cascade, an artificial waterfall, and the ruins of Leptis Magna. These ruins are the genuine article, an example of grand theft by the British Empire to embellish the King's garden! They originate from the ancient civilisation of Leptis Magna in Tripoli, North Africa where the local governor was persuaded that the Prince Regent, later George IV, could help himself to the ruins, much to the anger of the locals. After much difficulty with transportation these huge pillars eventually arrived in the park and were erected, recreating a little bit of ancient civilization in the leafy home counties.

Another strange edifice is the totem pole which stands proudly at the end of Canada Avenue, 100 feet of carved and painted Western Red Cedar. It was carved by Chief Mungo Martin and presented to Queen Elizabeth II in 1958 to commemorate the centenary of British Columbia being proclaimed a crown colony by Queen Victoria.

ABOVE: The Leptis Magna ruins.
MIDDLE: The lake.
BELOW: The waterfall.

The Totem Pole.

index